Ellen
STAY BROWN!
Con afecto de
Trinidad Sanchez
1995
cs

WHY AM I SO BROWN?

TRINIDAD SÁNCHEZ, JR.

MARCH/Abrazo Press
Chicago, Illinois

ACKNOWLEDGMENTS

Poems in this collection have been previously published in:
LA ONDA LATINA, 1985 & 1987; VIATZLAN INTER-
NATIONAL CHICANO JOURNAL, 1986; DETROIT CITY
ARTS QUARTERLY, 1988; WAYNE STATE REVIEW, 1988;
HORIZONTES REVISTA LITERARIA HISPANICA, 1990;
LA PRENSA NACIONAL, 1991 and EL CENTRAL, 1991.

Irene Vasquez, Francisco Tinajero, SVD, Jose L. Garza, Cecilia Mellado, Diana Alva, Sylvia
Sedillo, S.L., Daniel Rutt, Aneb Kgositsile, Lynn Walker, Linda Muir, Ivan Jenkins, Lolita
Hernandez, Ruth Ellen Cornwall, Guadalupe Lara, Cathy Figuera, Viola Chakmakien,
Christy Urgo, Dennis Brutus, Sadie Flennoy, and Nora Mendoza were inspiration for a
number of the poems—GRACIAS!

WARM ABRAZOS for Carlos Cumpián and Cynthia Gallaher whose
friendship and support have helped bring this project to completion. A very
special thanks for Martha Rodger, of Page Productions, who spent many
hours preparing the manuscript and for David Conklin, of Casa de Unidad,
for his consultation.

WHY AM I SO BROWN?, First Edition

For permission contact:
MARCH/Abrazo Press
P.O. Box 2890, Chicago, Illinois 60690

For additional copies write or call:
Mexican-American Cultural Center Bookstore
3019 West French Place
San Antonio, Texas 78228
1-800-368-5445

Illustrations: Carlos Cortez, Bill Day and Cheryl Phillips
Photo of Author: Bob McKeown
Cover Art: Nora Mendoza
Cover Design: George Perraza

ISBN 1-877636-03-7

CONTENTS

Dedicated to my carnal—
Robert L. Sánchez

bajo un cielo asoleado,
entre el granito
montañoso, desertoso,
lo sincero de Trino
es una cascada de imágenes
y virtudes humanas/sensuales ...

El Chuco, Tejas

Trenes del Trino

Garnered impressions on the
poems of Trinidad Sánchez, Jr.,
in "Why Am I So Brown?"

Poetry is often more than studied lines and structures, much more than the theoretical constructions so dearly beloved in academia—as are other arcane bits of archeological fluvia. Regrettably, much of the passion and emotional appeal of poetry has been sepulchred, as if song and lyric were to be beached on the shores of a logical set of logistics: things emplaced in their proper spaces, all neat.

Fortunately, there are those restless souls, those questing beings who sentiently prowl the vast spaces of our human capacity to question, to struggle, to articulate the pain and the celebration of our most natural humanity. It is to that sense of the most palpable, of the human happenstance, to that whitmanesque "barbaric yawp"—that jodazo chingonométrico—that cater-wauling bit of human-ness, that animate/spiritual self which strains at bars, chains, walls, fear, poverty, injustice, while also being enmeshed in the societal madness itself. Oh, yes, it is in response to the anger and love, the seeking of a divine purpose by Trino, it is to that question as to why there is even color in our thoughts that the poems cry out.

Though there is a strong and burning sense of "raza" in the poems, the most searing of questions confront the humanity in all sentient beings. There is thus a roughhewn poetic outcry, a searing canto which wails out a bluesiness cultivated in the backroads of an America that is also Chicana, a tierra which has felt the imprint of raza migrating to plant its seeds upon all horizons.

There is a heady sense of the actual in the poetry, a power fueled by experience, by pain known and dealt with, and the foundation is a boundless hope, a faith, a living testament to the love of people and persons, resulting in justifiable anger, impatience and resolution to act, to embrace and to struggle against the infirming mean-ness which seems to pervade our societal fabric—nationally and internationally.

Trino, the poet, sings the shaman song of meaning and justice, and the poems take on the trappings of outcries spoken in the verbs, nouns, and nuances of people who truly experience pain—not imagined or fantasied. It is truth, and it is palpable and authentic.

WHY AM I SO BROWN?

The urgent appeal to create "missionaries for the year 2000" inveigles the cynic to stop condemning humankind and to take on the struggle alongside women, men and youth against the perfidy of institutionalized society, against the cold corruption which starves humanity for the benefit of the few.

It is honestly felt pain, the integrity of experience, and the will to wage struggle so that poetry becomes a shield, an arm for defense and a tool to build a more humane world. Trino sings out the communal song of realization within the beautifying context of humanity, of those who labor in order to eat and shelter their families. It is a much needed song.

The questions posed have that rare passion of a poet surviving within the familial fold of his people—far from ivory towered halls, far from imaginative excursions into make-believe virtual pain. There is a resilient sense of actual people fighting marginal existence, daring to take back their dignity from the distorting laboratories of the institution. There is notable triumph against the pain of anomie, of alienation, as the poems burrow deep into existential outcries reverberating from barrio to barrio, and on to ghetto streets seeking of a humanity of many faces and voices.

Pride emanates from the lines, a pride which acknowledges the mortality of living things, and Trino rides upon the pride-express-train with a sensible embrace for all beings. There is room for everyone, even for those who have given up their rights to autonomy and empowerment, those who have opted for the staid and denatured existence behind ivory covered walls, in untidy yet contrived cubby holes.

"Why Am I So Brown?" the poet asks. A smile of self-affirmation threads its way forcefully, yet graciously, through poems written in cadence to life experienced and known, and the question is moot, answered by a reverberant song of celebration, of beauty within the humanity of Trino, his family, his friends, his people—and ultimately the grand humanity which is alive within all sentient beings. It is a tribute to life's meaning; a quest for making each moment count, meaningful.

Trino's work is a continuation of the vision and daring of those chicano poets who broke through the vapors and lies of a staid, academic racist society—he is the heir apparent of angered, caring poets like Abelardo "Lalo" Delgado, Nephtalí de León, Raúl R. Salinas, Heriberto Terán, José Montoya, and E. A. Mares—poets who spoke out strongly and courageously when doing so was dangerous.

It is a song of realization and an outcry which dares to confront the evil perfidy of institutional MAN...and it is a most moving poetics which has no need to be coy, pretty, nice, neat nor safe....

Ricardo Sanchez, Ph.D.
Performance poet/writer
and activist
El Paso, Tejas
5° de mayo de 1990

Reality is life and the other person. Once you forget reality you live in a vacuum with no amistades (friends). Amistades and having corazón are essential to the Chicano, Latino, Hispanic culture, to stay in touch with reality you have to stay in touch with your amistades, your family, even your enemies. You have to acknowledge and respect everyone.

A CHICANO THEOLOGY
Andres Guerrero, Th.D

ADENTRO EL CALOR DEL INVIERNO
(Inside the Winter Warm)

Voice: I

Recite a poem full of tenderness
one which reaches into my heart
uncovering the tears in my bosom ...
a poem to accompany this drink ...
one reaching into the interior of my soul
and which gleans the words of our philosophers,
protagonists and revolutionary heroes.

Recite a poem like a song born in struggle
verses which bloom from this reality
and from the dreams we all have of peace -
those which are full of the odors of Spring
the freshness of the flowers.

Voice: II

Te la canto, te la canto
está poesía llena de ternura
que te llege a tu corazón tieso, duro
lleno de lágrimas,
te la canto para acompañar
aquel trago de whiskey ...
uno de aquellos que llege
a lo profundo de tu alma
en el cual espican las palabras
de nuestros pensadores,
protagonistas y héroes revolucionarios.

Ahhhhh, te la canto
como una canción nacido en batalla
versos que brota de esos realidades,
y que surgen de los sueños,
que llevamos todos, por la paz-
la cual está llena del olor de primavera,
y la frescura de las flores.

Ahhhhh, lo cantamos juntos
adentro el calor del invierno
aquel tiempo de ser feliz y sonreír
calor de invierno, te esperamos pronto
porqué eres libertad, eres la justicia!

Ahhhhh, we will sing it together
inside the winter warm
a time of happiness - a time for smiles.
The warm of winter, we await your arrival
you are liberty, you are justice!

WHY AM I SO BROWN?

for Raquel Guerrero

A question Chicanitas sometimes ask
while others wonder: Why is the sky blue?
or the grass so green?

God made you brown, mi'ja,
color bronce - color of your raza, *your people*
connecting you to your raíces, *your roots*
your story/historia
as you begin moving towards your future,

God made you brown, mi'ja,
color bronce, beautiful/strong,
reminding you of the goodness
de tu mamá, de tus abuelas, *your grandmothers*
y tus antepasados, *your ancestors.*

God made you brown, mi'ja,
to wear as a crown, for you are royalty -
la raza nueva - the people of the sun.
It is the color of Chicana women -
leaders/madres of Chicano warriors
luchando por la paz y la dignidad
de la justicia de la nación Aztlán!

God wants you to understand ... brown
is not a color ... it is:
a state of being, a very human texture
alive and full of song, celebrating -
dancing to the new world
which is for everyone ...

Finally, mi'ja,
God made you brown
because it is one of HER favorite colors!

1986/1993

MI'JO

for Gene Páramo

Mi'jo
the brown skin body
the godson -
the son of gods -
our ancestors
the son I always wanted
the semilla -
the son of amistades
whom I love
the son
the gods sent to us
reminding us we are
La Raza Nueva
La Raza Cósmica
A Royal People
we are the
People of the Sun.
Mi'jo
your brown skin body
lleno de sonrisas,
I gather each one
into a bouquet of flowers,
flowers with eyes
listening - searching
calling - loving
flowers full of song,
lleno de sonrisas
I remember each one.

Mi'jo
the brown skin body
wrapping the gentle heart
of a young Chicano Warrior
I bless you …
the dreams of your childhood
I bless
your movement into manhood
I bless
the destiny calling you
I bless
yesterdays que son tus memorias
I bless
tomorrows que son tu futuro
I bless
today - the sonrisa of today
I bless …
Mi'jo -
my brown skin godson
I bless
mi ahijado - mi'jo
I bless you!

7/31/1989

CHICANO WARRIORS

For Andrew Daniel Mellado and
Matthew Hildifonso Mellado

On the edge
      this side of the new century
      this side of the year 2000
      this side of Primavera
      con el canto del gallo
      the gods break barriers of sound
      through darkness
      of cosmic time - the stars
      bursting forth - exploding
      celebrating once again
      nuestra ascendencia - our brownness
      la nobleza - royalty
      bronceando el futuro!
On the edge
      of worlds moving toward destruction
      pueblos en guerra
      sin espera - the gods renew our hope
      con nuevas esperanzas
      sending dos varones - twins - criaturas
      Matthew and Andrew
      to our midst.
This double birth
      brings us to the center
      del arco iris
      con nuevo horizontes.
      Celebrando: sharing blessings
      bendiciones for our new
      CHICANO WARRIORS!

Este doble nacimiento
    brings us to the center celebrando:
    poeming, dancing, singing nuevo cantos,
    telling his stories - her stories
    cuentos de los antepasados
    nuestra herencia,
    so, they will not be strangers,
    extranjeros in foreign lands.
    Celebrando la fiesta at the center -
    celebrando el futuro!
    We thank the gods
    we praise them
    for sending you to Vincent tu hermano,
    Vincent - father and Danielle their mother.
    We thank the gods
    we thank the heavens
    for blessing us
    la comunidad, la familia -
    raza noble y sencilla
    with strong and new
    CHICANO WARRIORS -
    Mateo y Andrés!

1/16/1989

HERE ARE TWO FACES LOOKING AT ME

In the distance, in the echoes of my mind
the canto de dos gallos rose to my consciousness
signaling the morning/singing songs of praise
to the gods of life/the gods of the living.

Here are two faces looking at me
dos caras - no podía escapar
la son y risa que brindaban.
Facing life is not too easy -
I can only live one day at a time ...
Here are two faces looking at me
full of historia/the future
like two stars from the cosmic galaxy.
Children, too young for words,
The music of their smiles
is what they use to describe
the compromiso, the compassion
deep in their hearts for the family
we all love/we all share.

Crazy - the sensation of twins
de la misma semilla
two faces sin máscaras - Suddenly
I see the children of the campesino
the children of El Salvador and Guatemala
I see the children of Nicaragua
I see the children of Detroit
I see the children of Aztlán
while the sounds of cultures clashing
surround me.

Double are the smiles - intense
driving me to places deep inside my heart
and the murmurs turn to drumbeats
calling on the clear vision/the new dreams
for remapping our homeland!

Detroit 12/1989

WHAT IS A CHICANO?

At the university
the question was asked again
called upon to reinterpret answers
I searched the sky to pray:
Diosito, por favor ayudame!
God, I could not see -
my bifocals failed me.
La conciencia was it turning old?
Anxiously, I turned to
my brown tenacious soul
for palabras hopefully you'd believe.
Surprise! My soul eluded me.

Regresando a mi pueblo
encontre la primavera
a celebración de colores
cantos del gallo
y los sonidos de mi barrio.
I saw the spirits of Chicano warriors
y Chicanas, mujers de su palabra
standing guard around the jardín
full of flowers - niños de sonrisa
all different shades of golden brown
colors of the arco iris in their eyes
dancing with their mothers,
dancing with their fathers.
Vi a mi abuelita Abigal y mi tío Fermin
descansando on the edge of this reality
their smiles chided me.
They seemed to say:
Do not be afraid of us. → *of your history. Of who you are*

What is a Chicano?
La pregunta turned into an echo
which surrounded me.
El calor, sol de medio día
warmed my heart
my pulse began to beat
drumsounds. I heard them sing
cantando canciónes nuevos -
trabajamos por la libertad
con hambre de la justicia
encontremos de nuevo la paz.

Returning to the barrio of my pueblo,
the question: What is a Chicano?
        did a somersault -
        Is it you? Is it me?

In the sky between LA & Detroit
2/1990

WHY AM I SO BROWN?

WHO AM I?

Am I -
the collection of pinto beans,
the pile of warm tortillas,
the chili relleno, the tostada chip
dipped in your salsa picante,
the flautas you eat with your dedos,
the chocolate con canela,
the nopales, the salchiches
you so richly savor?

Am I -
the orégano, the cilantro, la cebolla
of your salsa bien picoso,
the jalapeño pepper,
the pimiento in your gazpacho?
Let's be honest - it's true …
I did say: me gustan las gorditas!
I also said: I loved your chilaquiles!

Am I -
the super nacho of your life
or will I only be the rice and beans
forever?

staple. Main stay

Yo se bien, you don't like to joke around
at times you think of me as a taco de carbon!
Where's the beef? You would do well to teach
your mexican sandwich español
pa'que no pierde su identidad
and become Hispanic, better yet …
let him be CHICANO!

Sí, sí, I want to be
the pan de huevo you bite into,
the calabasa of your empanada,
the papa of your papa con huevos,
the sugar in your atole!
Ay, Mamacita!
the two of us are made for each other
like arroz con leche
the tamale wrapped in the oja
the extra queso on your enchilada …
and all you can say is:
    What's for dessert?

Detroit 6/15/1990

SOY CHICANA

I am a Chicana!
she stated …
something was lost in the translation
the others heard her say:
I am a radical militant!
I am a dangerous subversive -
a communist!
I am a brown feminist - wild & free!
I am a liberated Latina
a pistola-packing mama!
Someone whispered: There is no such word!
The bright red jalapeño earrings
were like quotation marks on her smile -
me hice preso de su sonrisa,
bien que picaba -
yo quedé queriendo ser
rey de su alma!
She made it clear
she believed - Mañana is NOW!
WE CANNOT WAIT FOR TOMORROW!
THIS *IS* AMERICA LATINA!
Mujer valiente, profesora,
a mujer de su palabra
she did not teach -
compartía the wisdom, the knowledge
of her abuelas y sus antepasados.
I am a Chicana!
she repeated -

y el guiñar de aquel ojo
told me she was much, much more ...
underneath her dark ebony skin
I was quite aware
she is my sister, my mother,
she is my father, my brother,
she is a lost dream found,
she is my past and my future.
I leaned toward her,
proudly whispered in her ear:
I am a Chicano!

12/10/1989

THE MEXICAN SANGWITCH

Is it a tortilla with peanut butter and jelly,
or jalapeños piled on Wonder Bread?
Is it a coney made with tortillas,
or a Kaiser roll smothered
with salchiches y salsa mayonesa?
Is it chorizo con huevo on whole wheat,
or refried beans on white bread?
Is it the patron saint of botanas,
or a Mexican who can only speak English?
Is it the same as an American Taco?
Is it a Mexican playing tic-tac-toe?
Is it carne asada on rye,
or guacamole on toast?
Do you really want to know why?
Is it me inside of you,
or you wrapped around me?
Is it a güera dancing with two Mexicans,
or two gringos putting the make on my sister?
Is it a super sandwich, with the official
ingredients labeled: HECHO EN MEXICO!
Is it a plain sandwich
made by authentic Mexican hands?
Is it true Juan de la Raza invented it?
Is it a moot question?
Are you a lawyer or a poet?
Does the judge really care?

Detroit 7/1990

BIENVENIDO

You have found your place
among the people,
Raza noble y raza cósmica,
ven a celebrar our brownness
… the place among the people
donde encontrarás a tí mismo
y la llamada a ser humano.

You have found your place
among the people and
you can always be 'en casa' …
echándote taquitos
tomando un traguillo.
A very special place
con los pobres y marginados
buscando la esperanza
y tratando la justicia.

You have found your place
among the people -
los que sufren soledad
pa' que compartas el hombro
organizando comunidad.
Oh, yes, my brother,
you have found your place -
prométeme, carnal, never, never
to trade places, pa' nada!

You have found your place
among the people
y a ellos se les pide
que siempre estén contigo
pa' que no pierdas el camino!
The place among the people
la familia, please remember:
I am you/we are one!

Yo también, Francisco
encontré a very special place
en lo profundo de mi alma
con estas palabras:
Pues, Hey! Francisco
BIENVENIDO! BIENVENIDO!

Detroit 7/25/1988

COMPARTIENDO DE LA NADA

Para aquellos que dicen:
¡Nada tengo/no tengo nada!

Compartiendo de la nada
        de la nada que tenemos
        y nada entienden los ricos.
Compartiendo de la nada
        se da lo que se puede
        y nos solidarizamos.
Compartiendo de la solidaridad
        nace la comunidad
        brota la justicia
        y se hace la paz!

SHARING OUR NOTHINGNESS

For those who say:
"I have nothing - I don't have a thing!"

Sharing of the nothingness
        of the nothingness that we have and
        nothing is what the rich understand.
Sharing of the nothingness
        we give what we can,
        we join in solidarity.
Sharing in solidarity,
        community is born
        justice blooms
        We make peace!

WHY DID YOU GO OUT TO CLARK PARK?

What did you go out into Clark Park to see?
A weed shaking in the wind? No?
Then what did you go out in Clark Park to see?
A Chicano shaking his weed to remove the bad seed!
A Chicano wearing fine tweed? No, those who wear
fine tweed are to be found in the Renaissance Towers!
Then what did you go out for?

Marta asked me to write a special poem
adding if she wrote it - well,
she has known José a long, long time
she'd become too emotional and cry -
as if José did not understand
the lágrimas from the heart -
so, I said: I'm macho, right!
I'll try!

José, I have not known your other life
nor have I known your exes
nor was I there for all the borracheras
or the eating out with enchiladas!
I want to make it clear - Orale!
I went out to Clark Park ...
I went out to see José Levy Garza
celebrating Chicano Literature con su libro
MASCARAS TACUACHITOS Y UN MONTON MAS
and a botella de tequila!

I went to Clark Park, ése
and found your mejicle spirit
walking out of pepino y tomate fields
shaking the dirt from cowboy boots.
I followed and watched your spirit
moving with the wind toward Clark Park
among the ganga de pachucos y camaradas
while gathering inspiracion
from new and worn-out dreams ...

I saw your spirit dancing
to the leftover Xicana/Salsa music
which hangs in the trees
like the morning mist -
the nectar of the gods!

I saw your spirit recording
sounds and words from echoes
of festivals past and other parties
en la madrugada, ése -
I found your spirit gathering
in colors and tiny bits/pieces
of memories of barrio life
for your collages.

Hey, José, I'll keep this short,
(let me borrow a line from your book)
"so the ice in your tequila
will not suffer from serious meltdown!"

The shooting at the Carnival Bar
in front of Casa de Unidad
distracted me for a moment,
so I asked, the viejito, as he sat
under the maple -
Perdoname Señor, have you seen
José Levy Garza, I mean ...
Have you seen his spirit?
He smiled and pointed
to the patch of sky
which covered Clark Park,
toward the one star
shining brightly
y con ganas!

Detroit 9/16/1989

DEATH OF A CHICANO WARRIOR

For SANTIAGO CHAVEZ (1934-1986)

Today, la hija consentida
me informó de las noticias
the sad news:
cruel death visited
a great Chicano Warrior!

What does one say to death?

Noble day/Honorable day
marked by a warrior's passing
from our midst ...
clear the mist!
Let the sun shine in -
to proclaim, to celebrate
the life of: our friend
            our father
            our abuelo
            our tío
            our compadre
            our carnal
            but most of all
            our Great Chicano Warrior!

Bury his body
in the consecrated holy ground
where Chiefs of Nations rest.

Bury his body with honor
let his life be a song ...
canto de un pueblo que lucha
por su liberación.

Bury his body with roses
so he will understand
and we will remember
his life was not in vain.

Bury his body among the just
for he was a peacemaker
committed to justice!

Bury his body
in gentle, gentle ground
so he can take his rest ...
cover it with lilies
reminders of the Resurrection
of humankind
for the new world - AZTLÁN!

Bury the Warrior's body of
Santiago Chávez ...
Vengan, mis hermanos/as
ven raza,
take up
    the struggle
    the battles
with the gentle spirit of this
Great Chicano Warrior!

1986

SPACE POEMS

I

The space between
Fall and Spring
contains frozen tears,
we call it snow.

II

The space inside
Spring and Summer
falls ever so gently
into winter.

III

The space between
Fall and Winter
is full of dead leaves
and ripe apples.

MAY I HAVE A COPY OF THE NEGATIVE OR TELL IT LIKE IT IS ...

Today, this cold January morning, 1988 (the Year of the Piano! -
according to my friend) six of the seven "Cepillos" gather to be
Kodaked and Pentexed as proof to all who will view these
photographs that we are all happy. Saben bien que - a photo is
worth a thousand poems! Yes, we all know the negative will not
capture the recuerdos, the differences between us, the untold and
telling stories of misunderstandings, arguments and pleitos which
are so much a part of being seven brothers ... instead the film will
preserve us all Smiling! There is a disadvantage in being the
youngest Cepillo, it is missing a lot of the historia, the blessings
and the buenos tiempos as well as the war stories of my carnales
I want to ask a lot of questions ... but there isn't time.
I remember papa, "Tempus Fugit!" he often quoted as if he were
a scholar of Latin! Serving coffee and pan dulce my carnal
announced: "You KNOW it isn't easy being brothers!"
loud laughter filled the small dining room, there seemed to be
agreement.

SMILE! Sonreían! for the camera, perspectives from the left,
right, and now the middle ... Smile! Say: Cheese! Say: Viva la
Revolución! ... that's it, Smile! Snapshots taken from different
angles taking us in without explaining the whole truth
of where we stood or sat on important issues.
Funny, I thought, how smiles are apolitical!

Olivia, the niece and the youngest, asks of the brother whose visit
brought us together for these photos: What is it like returning
home? It is a question which takes him by surprise. The others
know Pontiac stopped being his home many, many years ago.
I turn to listen for his response and he speaks: It's us ...
home is when I am with my brothers!

In my heart, I felt he was right. It was good for all of us to be home with each other if only briefly for this photograph. Pontiac, 186 Rapid Street was home for all of us at one time or another … years seem to take their toll and now as this chapter moves to other beginnings - Pontiac, the place we call home is now part of a photograph of the Cepillos: Fernando, Eddie, Raúl, Arturo, Larry, Trino (Mario could not be present) and for the other generations of los hijos de Sánchez!

Pontiac 7/21/1989

SONRISA SABOR CANELA

Como costumbre cristiana y corriente
vengo a tu casa muy caballero y contento
a celebrar con compasión los cincuenta
cumpleaños que has cumplido.

Claro, sí claro, créemelo, desde el cielo
traigo esta copla plena de consuelo
a mi hermana, la que tiene sonrisa sabor canela
y que la clasifico con calidad
más que una estrella de cine.

Complacido de cumplir, sin cobrar un cinco,
aquel deseo tuyo - de escribirte, no cuento
pero sí una poesía y no de la cantina o un colorado!

Cincuenta pa'algunas son tiempos confusos
y condenados, Caramba! Al contrario,
veo que cincuenta lo acercas como conquista
hechándote varias copas de Cuba Libre por cada
año - al otro lado de la conyuntura
y hacia los ochenta, noventa o cien!

La Lucy, como reina en gloria recién coronada,
te encontramos al centro
de tus hermanos, los "Cepillos,"
Papá siempre te consideró la querida consentida.
Ahora, eres costilla de Alfonso, mi cuñado
mamá de cinco y abuela de otras criaturas.

A celebrar los cincuenta estas certificado
a dar consejos sin cauterizar!
Siento, lo siento de no poder cantarte
una canción o corrido, mejor al buen callar
llaman Sancho!

Bueno, mi querida hermana, te acompaño
a celebrar los cincuenta años con mi cariño
corazón de un hermano y cotidianamente
agradezco a nuestro Dios,
por haberte puesto en mi camino!

WHY AM I SO BROWN?

CINNAMON-FLAVORED SMILE

Like the usual Christian custom
I come to your home a gentleman & content
to celebrate with compassion the fiftieth
birthday which you have completed.

Yes, Oh, Yes, believe me, from the sky
I bring this poem full of comfort
to my sister, who has a cinnamon-flavored smile
and whom I qualify with highest regard,
more than a movie star.

Pleased to complete, without charging a nickel,
your desire to write you not a story
but a poem not from the bar nor risque!

Fifty for some are confusing times -
and condemned, Wow! On the contrary
I see that you arrived at fifty as a conquest
drinking a number of Cuba Libres for every
year on the other side of the juncture
towards the eighties, nineties or hundreds!

Lucy, like a recently crowned queen,
we find you in the center
of your brothers, the "Cepillos,"
Papa always considered you his favorite,
Now you are rib of Alfonso, my brother-in-law,
mother of five and grandmother of other children.

To celebrate the fifty, you are certified
to give advice without correcting harshly!
I feel bad at not being able to sing you
a song or a corrido, better yet,
Silence is golden!

Well, my dear sister, I accompany you
to celebrate these fifty years with my love
heart of a brother, and daily
I thank our God
for having placed you in my path!

MY GIFT TO YOU

My gift to you is not a gift
but it is a gift ...
words from poems, a poem of words.
Poems do not come easy,
Poems come and go, but words linger ...
my gift to you is words,
not just any words - special words
which another poet used to describe
the women in his life,
the ones he lived for and whom he loved.
Words are my gift to you
in order that they might linger,
that you might give them life
in the same way
your abuela Sofía y mamá Lucy
give them life ...
     Prieta - Negra
     Tapatía - La Inocente
     Azteca de mucha ley
     pura india de Monterrey
     simpática - Morena
     fuerte - muy sincera
     no muy santa - pero decente
     sonreindo - la primera ...
Words are my gift to you -
not just any words,
special words ... let them linger in your heart,
in the seed should you choose
for them to be part of the life
you share with others
for the new world!

7/31/1989

When you arrive
at the center of the bridge
one can go three ways
backward forward or
dive into your own beliefs
to gain freedom
to enjoy choices and
celebration of the human spirit!

Julián Zamora Alva

PUENTES

llegando al centro
el puente se me cambió en reto -
un péndulo de tiempo
hacia atrás y adelante: decidí
sumergirmé a mis creencias,
me puse a competir con
        El Sol Azteca -
Allí, Allí
       a medio puente
me encontré con mí mismo
       la libertad!

Cierto! Cierto!
Celebrando el espíritu humano
      de la familia,
      de los antepasados …
llegando al centro del puente
regresé a tierras robadas,
      tierras santas,
bailando en la arena
y la lechuza me habla,
      me canta,
      me invita
a subir el puente
a empaparme con agua!

TRINIDAD SÁNCHEZ, JR.

SI DIOS QUIERE

A refrain I often heard
my mama say: Si Dios quiere!
(If God wants it to happen it will)
Mamá learned this from her mother
who after all must have learned it
from her mother, who probably
learned it from her mother or grand-
mother who learned it ...

Let's see if it's what God wants ...
I thought to myself, picking up the phone
I dialed God to ask: Is this what you want?
people on welfare,
children overdosing on drugs
killing each other with handguns?
Nicaragua overthrown by the Yankee government,
madres searching for los desaparecidos
a pope telling us not to be political
on his way to meet with generals?

Mamá continued making tortillas
as I waited on the phone.
Finally, in frustration I did
what every faithful son does to his mother
... trust her.
I asked: Do you think
God will ever answer the phone?
Mamá without breaking strokes of the palote
with which she rolled tortillas, said:
... Si Dios quiere!

FOR MAMA

(at the Nightingale Nursing Home)

Sitting here with you
holding your hands,
which so often moved in and out
against each other and in concert,
creating art out of balls of thread and yarn,
when not turning the masa to roll
the tortillas de harina,
(a tradition not learned now lost).
Tortillas which for all of us meant "home"!

Taking my hands into yours
you quietly study the hands of my timepiece.
How long has it been since you said:
I love you. I don't remember.
You know better than I how much time is left,
but the aphasia muffles your voice.
How much more time will it be
before papa returns to be with you -
I ask myself.

Gently moving your hands
which have so often prayed ave marias
I barely notice, I am holding yours again.
Holding back my tears of anger
unable to bring life to your right side
llamo a nuestro antepasado
the Tortonacos, Nahaus, the Zapotec people
especially los de Piedras Negras y Monterrey,
llamo al spiritu de Netzahuacoyotl for words
to gather the spirit of your tambora
with the sounds of the requinto y harana
para celebrar la fiesta de tu vida
while my heart prays to Tonaztin
and to Huehuetéoctl, the god of fire
to perform a miracle
to rekindle in you
the flame of life.

1990 Día de las Madres

DESDE QUE TE CONOCI

Sylvia - desde que te conocí
desde ese momento de nuestra amistad
(momento inovidable)
has sido una hermana
      mujer fuerte
y a la vez amable
      mujer de lucha
y a la vez sencilla
      mujer revolucionaria
y de su palabra.

Sylvia - mi hermana
has sido inspiración para aquellos -
      que sin guitarra -
cantan sus canciónes,
      sin lápiz
escriben poesía
      sin tinta …
pintan visiónes de aquel mundo
lleno de amor y de justicia.

Sylvia - has sido fiel a tu compromiso
invitando a tu hermana a acompañarte
a liberar a tu hermano
sabiendo bien que la mujer
no llega a ser liberada
sin la liberación del hombre -
de tu hermano.

Sylvia, querida hermana,
sigues siendo mujer de tu palabra
y yo sigo queriendo ser tu hermano!

THE RAIN FOR PARCHED LANDS

The rain upon the window
gentle sounds
reminding me of the weeping
of mothers
searching for their loved ones,
los desaparecidos …
más fuerte el sonido
of the rain upon the window …
the tears of loved ones
los desaparecidos
weeping for their mothers …
somewhere along the journey
the weeping/the tears
turn to sounds of gentle streams
bringing new life
to parched lands.

MONSEÑOR OSCAR ROMERO - PRESENTE!

Por cierto se presentó
con los pobres/los marginados
a traerles la buena nueva
y se presentó con los más pequeños
a conocer, escuchar, y compartir su vida.

Monseñor Oscar Romero - Presente!
por cierto se presentó,
se encarnó en el sufrimiento
de su pueblo salvadoreño.
Y se presentó como mensajero del Señor
a denunciar las injusticias
de la intervención del gobierno Yankee!

Monseñor Oscar Romero - Presente!
por cierto se presentó
como amenaza a las multinacionales,
a los militares/a los ricos.
Y se presentó como fiel cristiano,
persona de fe, comprometido con la justicia.

Monseñor Oscar Romero - Presente!
por cierto se presentó
a llamarnos a nosotros
como compañeros para hacer lo mismo,
por cierto agradecemos tu vida
aquí con nosotros
ayer, hoy y para siempre!

Monseñor Oscar Romero
PRESENTE! PRESENTE! PRESENTE!

NO

Blessed be the NO
NO to the exploitation of our youth
NO to the registration for the draft
NO to the killing of the poor
NO to Williams International
NO to Militarism
NO to the Military
NO to Starwars
NO to war
Blessed be the NO
Blessed be the NO
Blessed be the NO of Daniel Rutt
Blessed be the NO of all
who have taken stands -
NO they will not
allow themselves to be exploited
NO they will not
participate in wars
NO they will not
kill their brothers and sisters,
the family of humankind.
Blessed be their NO
Blessed be their NO
Blessed be their NO!
    They shall inherit the land
    They shall find peace.
    Justice will be theirs
    for the beginning
    of the New World!

1986

UNA INVITACION

"Ven amigo, qué te pasa
te invito a la cantina
a una copa de vino
acompáñame …
Cantinero - la botella!

… brindemos a Nicaragua
por su sangre derramada
en su lucha por la paz!

… brindemos a las ilusiones
la dignidad y la justicia
que brota en El Salvador!

… brindemos a la 'nueva canción'
de lucha y liberación
cantada por Quetzales
desde Guatemala - escucha bien!

… rindemos a las esperanzas
del mundo nuevo que nace en cantidades
en el dolor de aquellas madres -
tan sufridas - de los desaparecidos!

… brindemos a los sueños
de otras realidades
que celebra tanto niño
entre bombas y la guerra.

Ven amigo, ¿qué te pasa?
acompáñame a tomar esta copa de vino
por aquellos deseos que florecen
en tierra tan sagrada.

Ven amigo … ya sabes lo que pasa
a nuestros hermanos y hermanas …
brindemos el último traguito
a la familia tan humana!''

WHY AM I SO BROWN?

AN INVITATION

"Come, my friend, what's happening,
I invite you to the bar
for a glass of wine
accompany me ...
Bartender - bring us the bottle.

... we toast Nicaragua
for the blood she has shed
in her struggle for peace.

... we toast the illusions
of dignity and justice
which bloom in El Salvador!

... we toast the 'new song'
of struggle and liberation sung
by the Quetzales
of Guatemala - pay attention!

... we toast the hopes
for a new world which springs forth
in the pain of those mothers
who suffer so - of the disappeared.

... we toast the dreams
of other realities
celebrated by so many children
amidst the bombs and war.

Come, my friend, what's happening?
accompany me with a glass of wine
for those desires that are flowering
in this so holy earth.

Come, my friend ... you know what's happening
to our brothers and sisters ...
we toast the last drink
to the family that is so human!''

CELEBRACION FLOR Y CANTO

Al pueblo nicaragüense

Alba/la mañana
flor y canto
canto y flor.

Celebración
de
flor y canto
flor de justicia
cantos de liberación
flor y canto.
La justicia florece
el pueblo libre
canta
cantos de liberación.

Celebremos
Celebremos
una celebración,
las flores,
los cantos.
Un pueblo libre
celebra
sus flores y sus cantos!

Celebración
de la vida
flor llena de vida
vida llena de canto
flor y canto
celebración de colores
flores de colores
cantos de colores!

Pájaros en las flores
picaflores y sinsontes
pájaros que cantan
cantan, cantan
alegría, paz
liberación y justicia.

CELEBRATION OF FLOWER AND SONG

For the Nicaraguan people

Daybreak/the morning
flower and song
song and flower.

Celebration
of
flower and song
flower of justice
songs of liberation
flower and song.
Justice blooms
a free people
sings
songs of liberation.

We celebrate
we celebrate
a celebration,
the flowers,
the songs.
A free people
celebrates
their flowers and their songs!

Celebration
of life
flowers full of life
life full of song
flower and song
celebration of colors
flowers of colors
songs of colors!

Birds on the flowers
picaflores y sinsontes
birds that sing
sing, sing
happiness, peace
liberation and justice.

Pájaros
de
flor y canto
canto y flor
pájaros que celebran
celebraciones
de
flor y canto!

Atardecer/la noche
lleno de flor y canto
canto y flor.

Birds
of
flower and song
song and flower
Birds of colors
birds that celebrate
celebrations
of
flower and song!

Evening/the night
full of flower and song
song and flower.

O COME, O COME EMMANUEL

They wait for the war to end
they wait for their country to be invaded
they wait for the killing to stop
they wait for the massacres to cease
they wait in welfare lines
they wait in food stamp lines
they wait in soup lines
they wait for welfare checks
they wait for checks from social security
they wait for a room in the nursing home
they wait for filthy infested slum hotel rooms
they wait for empty boxes to live in
they wait for winter to go south
they wait on sidewalk grills for steam heat
they wait on street corners for a handout
they wait on the edge of reality for despair
they wait in bus stations without a ticket
they wait for a bottle of wine to kill the pain
they wait for cigarette butts for a smoke
they wait for holidays to be remembered
they wait for never-ending bureaucracy
they wait for the red tape to disappear
they wait for the trickle-down theory
they wait for the rich to share their wealth
they wait for garbage to be thrown out
they wait for Reagan's promises to be fulfilled by Bush
they wait for the judge to show them mercy
they wait for life on death row
they wait in jail to prove they're innocent
they wait in prison for a visit or a letter
they wait for miracles at the clinic
they wait for Jesus to solve their problems
they wait for someone to shake him from his sleep
they wait wishing they didn't have to wait …
    some wait for the revolution
    some work for the revolution
    in order that humankind will not have to wait …
    what are you waiting for?
    what are you working for?

MARTYRS BY MISTAKE EN CENTRO AMERICA
In memory of Arthur Fusco and companion 3/3/85

Arthur Fusco, 22 years old
a handsome man -
"the most striking thing is his smile -
it is as wide as his face!"
"He was very much like an enthusiastic
large little boy ...
when you met him he made you feel good,
exuberance, energy."
"He had many friends."

La mamá, his only mother, called him
"My masterpiece" - her very best!
Her BOY BLUE had become her PIETÁ.

Fluent in Spanish, he acted as interpreter
for those que no hablaban español
en Braus Laguna, Honduras.

The Pentagon called it "Civic Action!"
"FIRE IN THE HOLE IN 5 MINUTES ...
FIRE IN THE HOLE IN 4 MINUTES ...
FIRE IN THE HOLE IN 2 MINUTES ...
FIRE IN THE HOLE!"

There was no radio,
no way of hearing the warning over the noise
of a 35-horsepower motor.
There were no buoys marking the demolition site.

Falling down in bits and pieces,
Did Fusco think it might have been better for him
to have given his life para su gente de Nueva York!

Las noticias - the news is not clear,
no way of confirming it was his body!
Did Mike Uyeda, the Japanese American,
his companion,
recall the memorias of his ancestors,
memories of Hiroshima!

Martyrs by mistake …
maybe it was a mistake …
they entered the navy and
they did not refuse
to go to Central America.

Mistake or not,
ustedes saben bien -
igual que yo -
que ellos eran víctimas
de la intervención injusta
del gobierno Yankee
en Centro América!

Mistake or not
you know fully well -
the same as I -
that they were victims
of the unjust intervention
of the Yankee government
in Central America!

A WOMAN OF HER WORD

for Aneb Kgositsile

Like a gentle stream flowing
a quiet sunset falling
she is a woman of her word.
Like the Mary before her
who bore the Word
which nourishes the struggle
of those who hunger for Justice
and who bore the Truth
in her word
she is a woman of her word.
Like the Word which became human
para el pueblo/the incarcerated
los que no conocen
la justicia o la paz …
she is a woman of her word.
Mujer revolucionaria
taking up arms which are for loving
justice - peace and words
which strengthen the weak with life,
she is a woman of her word.
Blessed are the women.of their word,
blessed are the words spoken
by the women of their word.
Blessed are we who have known
such women,
women of their word!

Cheryl

STAND STILL MY FRIEND-LISTEN TO THE SONG

for Sr. Kit Concannon, S.L. 8/22/21 - 1/27/87

> "To be touched by living poetry
> can only make us better people."
> Haki R. Madhubuti-poet

Lucky me
the task
to write
a poem
without a kit
about Kit
for Kit
a
woman
whose life
is a poem
in
rhyme/sonnet
epic/haiku
free verse
a poem
a song
most of all a song
a poem song
inebriated with the suffering
of her brothers and sisters
a poem song
washed clean with hope
full of love in her heart
a poem song
for strengthening the weak
with life/with hope
a poem song
for hiding the wounded
from the wicked
a poem song
for standing with them
in solidarity
a poem song
singing the praises of
her lover/her God

a poem song
about friendship
for a new world.
Stand still, my friend
stand still
let your heart be quiet
and listen to the song
she sings it
for you/for me
for us
she sings her song
stand still my friend
listen!
listen!
to the song
Kit's Song.
Sing your song, Kit
your poem song
sing it, Kit
sing it loud
sing it clear
sing it long, Kit
long
real long!

THE INCONGRUENCIES OF LIFE
VS. RELIGIOUS RITUALS

Some read the sports page each day -
a ritual which is religious -
studying which of the false gods won
and the amount of money lost on wagers.

Some read the weather each day -
a ritual which is religious -
looking for information on whether
their crops will have a profitable harvest.

Some read the financial page each day -
a ritual which is religious -
reviewing their stocks
for high margins and dividends.

Some who cannot read
spend their mornings - Thanking God
(a religious ritual)
for having outlived bombs made in the U.S.A.

1986

IN MEMORIAM

Thomas Adams
Isidore Aikens
Gilitrea Amerson
James Anderson
Tyrone Anderson
Troy Armour
Floyd Armstrong
Keith Arrington
Tanisha Baldwin
Derick Barfield
Quinkela Baugh
Maurice Beckham
Ivan Berry
James L. Bivens
Robert Bostic
Demetrius Bradford
Reginald Bridges
Eric Burley
Johnny Butler
Ronald Carter
Julian Christopher
Alex Clay

Kevin Coleman
Darrel Crawford
Verita Crawford
Calvin Crossley
Billie Currie
Cecil Daniels
Gregory Davis
Leon Davison
Angela Dunbar
Tony Dunbar
Kyeisha Dye
Gerquarie Edwards
Lorenzo Fortner
Derrel Fowler
Gilbert Fox
Jurod Fulgham
Deandre Gilliam
Deanore Gillin
Walter Givens
Ryan Gordon
Isham Grady
Darryle Graham

Eric Harlan
Dorian Harris
Duwand Harris
Paul Harris
Lamar Hart
Latonia Hicks
Jeffery Hilson
Dennis Humphrey
Leonard Ingram III
Chester Jackson
Timothy Jackson
Paul James
Vonzie Johnson
Systhene Johnson
Don Jones
Stanley Jones
Dajuan Kelly
David Kelly
Calvin Kendricks
Tijuan Kidd
Kania Kirby
Shawn Landrum
Christopher Lee
Andre Lewis
Andrew Lewis
Roderick Lindsay
Trinia McCarty
Monyai McDanile
Rodney McRae
Cherle Malone
Rudolph Mark
David Matthews
Derrick Miller
James Miller
Marlin Miller
Kenneth Mitchell
Marlo Morales
Marvelyn Morgan
James Moore Jr.
Makeba Moore
Tommie Moore
Joseph Morrison
David Mullinax
Christopher Murray
James Newsome
Kenneth Newsome
Donna Olinger
Kenneth Phillips

Jarrel Philpot
Kent Raines
Kelly Rainy
Mitchell Ransom
Jeno Reed
Keith Reeves
Daniel Reyna Jr.
Ira Richardson
Kenyon Roberts
Anthony Robinson
James Robinson
Melody Rucker
Darlen Rudman
Robert Salter Jr.
Calvin Sanders
Clarence Scott
Colby Simmons
Angel Sistrunk
Cindy Sousa
Charles Stevenson
LaToya Stevenson
Andre Streeter
Duuna Leann Summers
Anthony Totton
Carla Ward
Jessie Washington
Tanisha Washington
Thomas Washington
Darryl Watkins
Charles Jesse Williams Jr.
Fred Williams
Jamella Williams
James Williams Bellinger
Orlando Williams
Shamel Williams
Thomas Williams
Victor L. Williams
Vincent Wims
Kimberly Winbush
Romale Winchester
Reginald Woods
Robert Woods
Darryl Ali Worley
Karla Woodward
Cornel Woody
Tarik Wright
Morgue No. 918

AGAIN - AGAIN/AGAIN
For Morgue No. 918

I hear the echoes -
sounds of jazz -
blowing through Detroit
for children whose voices
will never-ever play again.

Listen to the echoes
words of children's voices
blowing through the city
songs they will never-ever
sing again.

I hear the echoes
sounds of Uzis - handguns
tearing flesh/breaking hearts
of children playing in the wind,
I hear them again - again/again.

Listen to the echoes
sounds of mothers/fathers
somewhere in the wind
crying/weeping for their children
I hear them again - again/again.

I'm listening for the echoes
of this year coming to an end,
the warm autumn wind is leaving me
with thoughts of new Spring
and the resurrection
again - again/again.

7/29/1988

LET US STOP THIS MADNESS

Derek Barfield brutally died - brutally died
Clarence Scott brutally died - brutally died
Chester Jackson brutally died - brutally died
a hundred kids brutally died brutally died
brutally died brutally died

S.O.S.A.D. (THE WAR ZONE)
Errol Henderson

The bullets from the guns
that massacred the invalids
in San Miguel, El Salvador,
the bullets from the guns
that killed the poet
in Johannesburg, South Afrika,
the bullets from the guns
that kill the actors on TV,
for no other reason
than our own enjoyment,
are the same bullets
from the same guns
that kill the children
in Detroit, Michigan.
The bullets from the guns
that killed Martin Luther King, Jr.,
that killed Mahatma Gandhi,
that killed Oscar Romero,
are the same bullets
from the same guns
that kill the children
in Detroit, Michigan.
When will it stop?
When will we learn
to listen to the artists
teaching the children
songs of life
songs of liberation?

Let the children
grow into man/womanhood.
Let us stop weeping
for the invalids in San Miguel,
for the poet in Johannesburg,
for the children in Detroit.
Let us take a stand,
let us stop the bullets
from the guns
that kill our children.
Let us stop teaching
the children
that the bullets from the guns
are the only way
to deal with life.
Let us destroy the factories
that make the guns
that shoot the bullets
that kill our children.
Let us take a stand
to share life,
to break bread
with each other.
Let us stop this madness ...
the bullets ...
the guns!

Postscript:

As one of his last acts, the day after
Patrick Purdy machine-gunned five
children to death and wounded dozens
of others in Stockton, Calif., Reagan
pardoned a guy convicted in Texas of
illegally selling machine guns.

BY LARS-ERIK NELSON
Tribune Media Services Inc.

SHATTER THE PAST

Shatter the past
its composition
con amistades …
mother/child
todas las naciones
bring them together
their bodies/souls
a tierras robadas
por Cristóbal Colón
y re-robadas
por otros ladrones
de la historia.
Shatter the past
with circles of womyn
mujers de Atzlán,
America Latina
by remapping anew …
the shattered past.
La historia
must not repeat.
Hoy, es el comienzo
de la nueva epoca
la nueva primavera
el año 2000.
Shatter the past
on canvas
con circulos de mujeres
madres de los campesinos
de los desaparicidos
madres quienes lloran
por sus criaturas,
las que con su pecho
dan vida
y las revolucionarias.

Shatter the past
in real life
with circles of womyn
who against all odds
cry for justice
con corazones
lleno de amor.
Highlight our liberation
become our freedom
turn primary colors
into canciones y bailes!
Shatter the past
with its shadows
YOU can no longer
be the mujer dormida.
Shatter the past
with the arco iris
of primavera …
Take me with you!

9/8/1990

EL FUTURO - HACIA EL AÑO 2000

Un mundo nuevo
donde haya profetas
pensadores/revolucionarios,
donde todos sean poetas
escribiendo poesías, cantos de amor,
paz y justicia.
Que celebren los niños
con su son y canto -
niños con alegría,
niños que celebran
su liberación
con los presos.
Que los presos sean libres
como los niños
y que canten y gríten
cantos de liberación
con los niños.
Que la vida
sea un festival -
festival de alegría y justicia.
El mundo nuevo
donde no habrá ricos
ni bombas o guerras,
donde el único hambre
será por la justicia
todos seremos pobres
al fondo bien humano
llenos de cantos
celebrando
celebraciones de paz,
de justicia -
celebraciones de
un mundo nuevo
un nuevo mundo!

THE FUTURE - TOWARD THE YEAR 2000

A new world
where there are prophets
philosophers/revolutionaries,
where everyone is a poet
writing poems, songs
of love, peace, justice.
Let the children celebrate
with their sing and song,
children of happiness -
children that celebrate
their liberation
with the prisoners.
Let the prisoners be free
like the children
let them sing and shout
songs of liberation
with the children.
Let life
be a festival,
festival of happiness and justice.
The new world
where there will be no rich
nor bombs or wars,
where the only hunger
will be for justice,
everyone would be poor
fully human
full of songs
celebrating
celebrations of peace,
of justice -
celebrations of
a world that is new,
a new world!

UNBROKEN HEROES

Breaking Rocks
    to brake young men
    to brake old men
Breaking Rocks
    to brake their backs
    to brake their souls
Breaking Rocks
    to brake their dreams
    to brake their lust
Breaking Rocks
    to brake their songs
    to brake their fists
Breaking Rocks
    to brake their bodies
    tattoos are not enough
Breaking rocks
    to brake their hearts
    bullets could not brake
Breaking Rocks
    to brake their words
    to brake their poems
Breaking Rocks
    to brake their laughter
    to brake their love
Breaking Rocks
    to brake a nation
    to brake a people
Breaking Rocks
    to brake the notion
    of all of us
    Breaking Bread
    of all of us
    Breaking Bread
    of all of us
    Breaking Bread!

10/14/1989

MISSIONARIES FOR THE YEAR 2000

Men and women working with the poor
for their liberation touching the pain
in their struggle for freedom.
Prophets sharing their lives and
denouncing the unjust economic order
of the rich who exploit the poor.
Brothers and Sisters standing
in friendship with the marginated
of our society to advocate for change,
for justice and those looking toward
their own empowerment.

Men and women of their word like the Word
which became human in order for the blind
to see the poor. Brothers and Sisters
committed to building communities
where liberty is proclaimed to captives,
where the rich are sent away empty,
prisoners are set free sharing the good news,
singing songs of justice/peace/love
songs of liberation.
Angels without wings - revolutionaries
taking up arms which are for loving and
announcing the good news - faith begets
justice begets faith begets justice!

Men and women liberated by their own struggle
to see the poor touching their pain and
remaining a sign of hope with those
whose hope is all but lost,
while dying a thousand deaths
with their own pain of lost hope
and unbelief in a gospel
which is not easy by human standards,
but rises from the struggle, for the resurrection
of the new world, - where there are no rich,
instead we are all poor - strong in hope -
full of love
shouting, crying out songs of justice ...

These are the followers of Sojourner Truth
Rutilio Grande, Dorothy Day, Oscar Romero,
Fannie Lou Hamer, Rosa Parks, Steven Biko,
Nelson Mandela, Dr. Martin Luther King, Jr.,
Dolores Huerta, César Chávez and Jesús.

These are the missionaries
moving from the now
toward the future
preparing for the new century
in the year 2000!

RECUERDOS DE LA AMISTAD

Recuerdos de la amistad
son los tiempos que pasamos juntos,
son las palabras compartidas
"amor tanto que te quiero,"
Recuerdos de la amistad
son las lágrimas en mi pecho,
los momentos que me siento sólo,
son los abrazos que nos dimos,
son las copas de vino
que brindamos ...
lo único que alivia el dolor
tan profundo en mi corazón
son los recuerdos de la amistad ...
y las rosas que brotan
en diciembre.

MEMORIES OF FRIENDSHIP

Memories of friendship
are the times we spent together,
are the words we shared
"Amor - I love you so!"
memories of friendship
are the tears in my heart,
the moments I feel alone,
are the embraces we gave each other,
are the glasses of wine
we toasted ...
the only thing which will alleviate the pain
so deep in my heart
are the memories of friendship ...
and the roses which bloom
in December.

TRINIDAD SÁNCHEZ, JR.

FESTIVATING FORTY

Forty can be failure
or mostly friends
with which to flirt and fornicate.
Fortitude is not a four-letter word
but it does keep one feisty at forty.
Feeblemindedness, facelifts,
fleshiness, and forty
should remain a fantasy!
Festivating forty years
of flaming hair color
should be a festival
with fanfare on film, so
when you're eighty
you will not forget
those fascinating days
in which you were surrounded by
fellowship, folly, flowers, fondness,
foolishness, foxiness, fireworks,
favors and flavors.
Festivating forty years
signifies you may continue to be a poet/ess
who is free speaking, free thinking,
free versifying, free wheeling, foul-mouthed
and full of furies -
writing fiction, fables, poetry
full of four-letter words like
folly, femininity, fleshpots, first nights of
fixations and freakishness.
Festivating forty
without fanfare or fandango, fireworks,
feeling, fervor, flashes, flora & fauna
is not fanaticism but foolishness.
This started out to be a birthday greeting
full of fancy finesse, fondness, fascination
forthrightness - without being flashy and
forceful ... Happy Birthday, Baby!

I KNOW WHAT SHE KNOWS IS
THAT SHE KNOWS WHAT I KNOW

She wanted to know
the secrets bottled up inside,
things revealed
only to my shadow.
She wanted to know
differences between
puppy love and human love -
If I loved others if others loved me,
most of all - did I love myself?
She wanted to know
differences between sex and love ...
I thought she knew!
She wanted to know
my sex, my age
to know if I was old enough
my grey hairs - she wasn't sure.
She wanted to know
the whole story -
a history of my living
and did I love my life
without a wife?
She wanted to know
things too difficult at times
for the mind to understand and know.
I did not have the words
to explain those things -
only the heart understands and knows.
She insisted on knowing ...
so, I took her hands
and gently placed them
on my heart!

1986

SURE SMELLS GOOD OR DID SHE MEAN ME?

Glancing into the kitchen, she said:
Sure smells good!
Was it the frijoles cocidos con cerveza,
my refried beans? Or did she mean me?
Was it the chorizo con huevos, flavors,
aromas impossible to imitate?
Or did she mean me?
Was it the tortillas toasting on the comal?
Or did she mean me?
Was it the jalapeño which when freshly cut
burns the tenderness of hands unaccustomed
to cooking? It may have been the fresh
oregano mixed with cebolla . . .
the salsa picante! Or did she mean me?
Con la canción: SABOR A MÍ in the background
I remembered the words of the Chicano
philosopher famoso, who said:
Eres lo que comes! - which roughly translated
means - You are what you eat!
Quietly walking away, I heard her say:
Sure smells good!

MY LOVER

She ...
was in such a hurry
to be at my side
She ...
spent the extra money
from her cookie jar ...
She ...
took a transatlantic flight
supersonic jet
first class
across town ...
She ...
got a little angry
I wasn't home!

1986

SONGS FOR POEMS OR VICE VERSA

She sang me a song entitled:

I WANT SOME REAL RECREATION!

I wrote her a poem with two titles:

COME HOME WITH ME - I'LL SHOW
YOU MY PERSONAL PLAYGROUND!

COME HOME WITH ME - I'LL SHOW
YOU MY ENTERTAINMENT CENTER!

1989

LOVE POEM # 46 or
LAS GANAS DEL GALLO

Las ganas del gallo en la madrugada -
tantas ganas que tiene le hacen cantar:

A nombrarte Justicia,
de sentir tu cuerpo junto al mío
y decirte "el amor nunca termina …"
de nombrarte La Paz
de sentir tu entrega igual que la mía
y decirte "te quiero" no tiene olvido.

Las ganas de nombrarte La Vida
cuando veo tu sonrisa y me hace reír
de llevarte al río a jugar todo el día …
de llevarte conmigo a callar la tristeza
que tanto la siento, tanto me friega
y saber que no es continua!

Ay! Mamacita - las ganas que tiene
el gallo tan temprano en la mañana!

6/1989

THE LAST ROSE IN THE GARDEN

I recall it was in October
the end of summer, the edge of autumn.
Inside her office I was admiring
the beautiful red rose on her desk
she said: it is the last rose from my garden ...
but I remembered the first time
we undressed each other with our eyes
and promised we would meet again.

She offered me the last rose from her garden
as I remembered the first time
we undressed to break the sixth and ninth
at the time, she laughed saying:
it was a two-for-one offer I could not refuse.

I accepted the last rose from her garden
recalling the first time
and my fantasy that
roses should last forever!

1988

CAUGHT
BETWEEN THE SHEETS
OF TWO LANGUAGES

This chilly weather reminds me of the poem
on the bed the other night. I used it for a sheet.
I pulled it up over me - it felt warm and sensual
as it rubbed against my calves and thighs
What a unique sensation to be fully covered by
a poem, una sabana. The poet of two languages
caught between the sheets, so to speak ... and
I was lost for words to describe the fantasy
of poems used as sabanas. I rolled over caught
without my static guard, the poem stuck to me -

we became one, the poem and I.

The words close to my chest agitated my heart,
my body temperature rose, I felt the sweat run
down my leg, on my chest, the more I moved to un-
ravel, the more it enmeshed its folds around me.
Clearly, it wasn't any ordinary poem printed
on linen paper, but rather a texture more like sexy,
sensual, silk. Eventually, I came loose
of its entanglement. How sweet it was!
I'll never understand how the words clung
to my body like hickeys! Sabanas queridas ...
What did you say? You think this poem
... is a lot of sheet?

2/14/1991

POST OFFICE DECISIONS

I went to mail your love letter -
How much will it cost? I asked.
He said: How much does it weigh?

How to measure love? I thought
recalling words carry weight.
I smiled ... under two hundred pounds!

How long will it take? I inquired.
He said: Depends how you send it!
First Class often takes three todays,

Special Delivery is the same ...
And all this is not guaranteed!
But ... will it arrive tomorrow?

Only if she is at home! he mused,
And you decide to send it!

WHY AM I SO BROWN?

NEEDING TO BE LOVED
IN THE VICTORIA ROOM

The rings and bracelets she wore
were her way of hiding
the wrinkles on her hands -
which revealed her age - an item
she did not wish to share.
The sparkle in her hair
was actually glitter from a 5 & 10 -
it somehow distracted me
from her inner beauty.
She whispered in my ear:
I want to sleep with all the famous poets!
in my mind, I said: Someday -
(I'll be a famous poet!)
It was the beer which revealed
in a voice too loud for the Victoria room
the pain of lost love, separation and rejections.
Lost in the past - trying to forget
groping for the future without strategy
or a man - she took another drink
needing to be loved.

OJOS NEGROS

El parpadeo de aquellos
Ojos negros
    son de Lupe Lara
    mujer de San Antonio
    y Grito de Mi Raza ...
    hoy te festejamos en el día de tu santo.

Ojos negros ...
    dicen "que los ojos negros no engañan!''
    así dice la gente.

Ojos negros
    de aquella sonrisa
    llena de música ...
    quisiera ser un Miguel Angel
    para pintar los ojos tuyos
    aquella mirada que me das y que llena
    lo profundo de mi corazón.

Ojos negros ... me recuerdan de mi niñez
    los pleitos en los juegos de canicas
    por aquellos 'ojos negros'
    que siempre los perdí!

Ahora yo más grande y viejo
    sigue la suerte mía,
    con aquellos ojos negros
    que tanto los quería!

12/12/1987

BLACK EYES

The twinkle of those
Black eyes
    belong to Lupe Lara
    a woman from San Antonio
    and The Cry of My People ...
    today, we celebrate your namesday.

Black eyes
    they say "black eyes do not deceive!"
    that is what the people say.

Black eyes
    of that smile
    filled with music ...
    I would like to be a Michelangelo
    to paint your eyes
    that smile which you give me and which fills
    the depth of my heart.

Black eyes ... they remind me of my childhood,
    the fights during the games of marbles
    for those "Black Eyes"
    which I always lost!

Now I, much wiser and older,
    my luck continues ...
    with those black eyes
    which I've desired for so long!

CATHY …

Cathy …
me pides una poesía/canto
y no encontré en mi *Cassell's*
las palabras para explicar
cómo tu sonrisa llega a mi corazón
entumecido …

Busqué en *Webster's Internacional*
palabras en inglés que me dijera
cómo captar tu alma
que baila al ritmo del viento
en la orilla de tu isla tan amada …
y no las halle.

Pedí a *Velásquez* que me dijera tal frase
para escribir una poesía enamorada
y le faltaron las palabras …

Junté varios diccionarios …
llegué a dudar de mi identidad de poeta
yo … ¿quién soy yo?
para escribir de cosas tan hermosas.

Mejor, aprecio tu presencia
como hermana y amiga,
la amistad que brindas
como sol de nuevo día
que me fortelezca en los momentos
que me siento sólo.

CATHY ...

Cathy ...
you ask me for a poem/song
and I did not find in my *Cassell's*
the words to explain
how your smile reaches my hard heart ...

I looked in *Webster's International*
for English words to tell me
how to capture your spirit
which dances to the rhythms
of the wind and the waves of the shore
on the edge of your beloved island,
and I could not find them ...

I asked *Velásquez* to give me a phrase
to write you a love poem,
and it did not have the words ...

I gathered various dictionaries,
I came to doubt my identity as a poet
I ... Who am I?
to write of such beautiful things.

Now wiser, I appreciate your presence
as a sister and friend,
the friendship you share
like the sun of each new day
giving me strength in the moments
which I feel alone.

SHEDONTWANNABECHICANA

Her great, great grandmother
escaped being sacrificed to the gods
by the most high priest,
she had some tías who resisted.
Netzahuacoyotl, a Chicano poet
wrote poems to women like her abuela.
Chichén Itzá/Uxmal were designed/built
by her grandfather and cousins.
She loves men with bigotes,
she had ten brothers and ten sisters.
She likes her beans refried con queso
she prefers corn tortillas to white ones
… always has.
Sometimes her tongue is in cheek
her words turn to barks without a bite.
The weekly trips to her hairdresser
and manicurist has them guessing …
Is she? or Isn't she?
The blood in her runs thick, full, red
it is connected with the sangre
(y la sangre no miente)
of her Mayan/Aztecan sisters
from her not too distant past.
El guiñar de aquellas ojos azuelas, surely
she has been a goddess in another life.
Given all the right ingredients
to hecha un grito which will put
la famosa Lucha Villa to shame.
Her huraches are worn out from dancing
polkas, rancheras, cumbias, any type
of música with a taste of salsa.

My compadre whispered to me:
disafortunadamente (very unfortunately)
she is a doñawannabe, so taking my cue
I lifted my tequila en mano -
I toasted this beautiful woman
who chur look like, but according
to my compadre is a doñawannabee,
pero in reality, we all know ...
    en el mero de su corazón
    She IS a CHICANA!

1991

IMAGENES

Viola,
Güerita de mi vida
adelante/fuerte
como postre delicioso
con café cappucino.
Amor, de esa cara de porcelana
que no se quiebra
sería difícil recomponer los pedazos.

Christy
ojos de cristal, pelo rubio
flor Italiana de primavera!
Bien sincera, qué te doy/qué me pides?
Tacos a mi manera, frijoles de la cazuela?
Güerita bailadora, qué esperas?
Toca la música ranchera/salsa …
prometo no pisar esos pies tan finos
esos zapatos de cristal!

Güeritas
la amistad no explica el amor
que sentimos por la sonrisas
que comparten con sus amigos.
Flores violetas de cristal
mujeres fuertes de celebración
vidas lleno de amor
piden poesías del poeta -
qué les rezo, qué les canto?
Palabras no explican amistades.

IMAGES

Viola
the blond one of my life
assertive/strong
like delicious dessert
with coffee cappuccino.
Love, your porcelain face
don't let it break -
it would be difficult to reassemble.

Christy
crystal eyes, blond hair
Italian flower of Spring
Favorite one, what will I give you,
what do you ask for?
Tacos my way, beans from the pot?
My dancing blond one, why are you waiting?
The ranchera/salsa music is playing ...
I promise not to step on those beautiful feet
those crystal shoes!

Blond ones
Friendship does not explain the love
we feel for your smiles
you share with friends.
Violet flowers of crystal
strong women of celebration
lives full of love,
you ask for poems from the poet
what shall I recite, what shall I sing?
Words do not explain friendship!

GÜERITAS

To las güeritas in and out my gate
las que pasan por las puertas
comprometidas y muy fuertas
my, oh my, why do you hesitate?

Bien chulas in and out my door
my love for you has left me poor
me vuelvo loco, you only ask for more.

Queridas on the elevator
the Chicanas call me "traitor!"
Esas güeritas in and out my casa
por favor, forgive me raza!

Preciosas in and out my life
why is it not one wants to be my wife?
Las que van y vienen - no más les pido:
"no se detengan!"

Aquellas rubias in and out my heart
without you my life falls apart
las que van in and out my home
me quitan feelings of being alone!

Las mamacitas up and down the stairs
las muy necias ... que se vayan
con Julio Iglesias!
Las que pasan por las ventanas -
VENTANAS! VENTANAS!
Hey, ese Trino, si tiene ganas!

NO ES LO MISMO
(It is not the same)

Falling out of love and
falling out of a plane
are not quite the same ...
so, I fastened my seat belt!

1987

WHY DO MEN WEAR EARRINGS ON ONE EAR?

¡Sepa yo!
Maybe por costumbre, maybe porque es la moda
or they have made promesas, maybe for some vieja
for cosmetics or because some women love it
because they were on sale
because they are egocentric cabrones y buscan la
    atención
because la chica selling them was sooooo mamacita
and they could not refuse
maybe to tell you they are free, innovative,
    avant-garde
and liberated, maybe because of the full moon
because one earring is cheaper than two
maybe to keep the women guessing
and the men on their toes
maybe they are gay caballeros
maybe as a reminder de algo que no querían
    olvidar-
like the last time they had sex or to be sexy-
    looking
maybe they are sexually confused
maybe to let *you* know they are very easily
    sexually aroused
maybe to separate themselves from los más machos
maybe they are poets, writers
y la literatura is their thing!

Why do men wear earrings on one ear?
¡Sepa yo! Maybe baby ...
they are reincarnated pirutos of yesteryear
maybe they lost the other one
maybe they are looking for someone good at cooking
maybe it makes them look like something is cooking
maybe to send signals - the left ear is right
and the right ear is wrong
maybe it depends on which coast you are on.

Why do men wear earrings on one ear?
Who knows … maybe it looks much better
than the nose, the toes
maybe to remind others which ear is deaf
maybe to distinguish them from those who don't
and those who won't,
maybe to separate them from the women
maybe because as some women say:
men can only do things half right
maybe to be imitators of the superior sex -
        half way
maybe they are undercover policía trying to be
        real cool
maybe they are Republicans trying to be
progressively liberal
maybe they are Democrats disguising their
        conservatism
or leftists telling you they are in the right party
or revolutionaries looking for a peace - P E A C E!

Maybe they are undecided
maybe to be cute
maybe because life is short.

Why do men wear earrings on one ear?
¡Sepa yo!

POEMAPHOBIA

Are you really poemaphobic
you think the only good poet
is a dead poet!
Are you really poemaphobic
because I have a poem
just for you!

Are you afraid
my Chicano español, querido lenguage
of all the niños and their gods
will become the official language
or my brown canela-colored words
will rub off on you and give you
a deep brown cocoa-colored tan or
you will turn into a bi-lingual
bi-cultural, bi-lateral, bi-sexual
person with a little picante
in your step.

Tienes miedo
que no lo vas a intendar
por el simple razón
eres un baboso without any rhyme
y la policía will ticket your meter
or the Detroit judge will not understand
what poetic justice is?

Are you afraid
the music in the words, the corrido sonido
mixed with the Mexican Mora jazz
will shake loose your bones, you just might,
stand up, undress fully naked in public
start to dance, to jitterbug
with some salsa in your cumbia!

Are you afraid
my political poems will enter your
left/right - right/left brain
you might revolutionize your thought,
change right then and there,

liberate your spirit, expand your mind
change your faulty thinking, uncover the lie
you have lived all these years,
or in some capitalistic manner
you will be enriched/not know how to bank it
lose some money on my account!

Are you afraid
of actually breaking down crying
breaking open the vein in your forehead
putting some rise in your blood pressure
tightening up your ass, vomiting in public
falling over with cramps and your claustrophobia
will reappear, rip you apart, open the pain -
be like salt on old wounds, incite a riot
in the hurt hidden deep in your soul.

Are you afraid
of the black poet how he might kill you
with his blackness, suck you into the deep hole
of his poem, that you'll have to listen to him
for the rest of your life
or you might return niggerized and
all your white friends will disown you
call you a ... ... poem lover!

Are you afraid
you will realize
the distance you must travel
to be fully human is the path
from the brain to your heart
and it will take a poem a day
until you die!

7/1/1991

STOP ABORTIONS

Detroit, Michigan
on the John Lodge Expressway
the billboard dutifully reminds
travelers to and from work and home:

STOP ABORTIONS

Yes, we must stop abortions
I thought to myself …
to allow these babies to grow up
in order to send them to wars
in foreign lands to kill babies;
to allow them the luxury
of struggling all their lives
in the ghettos, barrios and on
the margins of our society.

Yes, we must stop abortions
I thought to myself …
to allow these babies to grow up
to be the poor and unemployed
of our cities;
to allow these babies to become
our cross addicted dope heads
and junkies of our society!
To allow these babies to have babies
in order for them to grow up
marinating in our living cemeteries
(the jails & prisons) at overcapacity!

Oh, yes, we must stop abortions!
I told myself ...
in order to allow these children
the right to life!
These babies have a right
    to bear the burdens
    to carry the cross
    to struggle
    to be free
    in a land
    of democracy!

1984

WHICH SIDE DO I TAKE?

Which side do I take?

Any side

the other side

the left side

the right side

the wrong side

the correct side

the up side

the down side

Is the middle a side?

God's side

the devil's side

alongside

the outside

the inside

side by side

sideways on

the sidewalk

the poor side

the rich side

the gay side

the straight side

the democratic side

the republican side

the happy side

the angry side

the religious side

the atheist side

the radical side

the apathetic side

the revolutionary side

the pacifist side

the greedy side

the cooperative side -

Homocide? Suicide?

you can be on the outside

looking in - or on the inside

looking around!

Frequently asked: Come on Trino,

you do get a little on the side?

Often reply: It's been so long …

I didn't know they moved it to the side!

Which side do I take?

Which side are you on? …

Excuse me ?

Which side are you on?

Sorry … that will take another poem!

THE POET'S DILEMMA

To say:

The space between
our hearts
will never separate us!

or

The space between
our hearts
is full of love!

... when men are friends they have no need of justice,
while when they are just they need friendship ...
                                                    Aristotle

Trinidad Sánchez, Jr. originates from Pontiac, El Michoacan del Norte, Michigan. He is the ninth of ten children born to the late poet Trinidad V. Sánchez and Sofia Huerta. He spent the early twenty-seven years of his life with the Society of Jesus as a member of the Detroit Province of Jesuits.

He has been recognized for his activism on behalf of those in the penal system and his involvement in peace and justice issues with the Dr. Martin Luther King KEEP THE DREAM ALIVE AWARD.

Trinidad has been featured as guest poet and lecturer at Beyond Baroque Literary Center, Venice, CA; at The First Nezhualcoytl Poetry Festival, The Mexican Fine Arts Center Museum, Chicago, IL; and The Detroit Institute of Arts Lines Series as well as several universities including Wayne State University, Detroit, MI; University of Wisconsin, Madison; Cal Poly Tech, San Luis Obispo, CA; Bowling Green University, Bowling Green, OH and other academic and community centers.

For the past ten years he has been actively involved with two popular poetry venues in Detroit—H.I.P. (Horizons In Poetry) and the Latino Poets Association. His essays, literary reviews and poetry have been published in several anthologies and alternative press publications.

He served on the editorial committee for the first anthology of Detroit Poets, LA ONDA LATINA EN DETROIT. His most recent works include AUTHENTIC CHICANO FOOD IS HOT!, COMPARTIENDO DE LA NADA and two volumes of poetry by father and son, POEMS BY TRINIDAD V. SANCHEZ & TRINIDAD SANCHEZ, JR. He lives and works in San Antonio, Texas with his wife Regina and daughter Amanda.

Information regarding Poetry Performances and Lectures contact: Trinidad Sánchez, Jr., 1443 West Rosewood Ave., San Antonio, Texas 78201, (210) 735-2560.